SHAME POINT ZERO

SHAME POINT ZERO

A Collection of Poetry
and Spoken Word

PJ

PHOENIX JAMES

SHAME POINT ZERO

First Edition: 2023

ISBN: 978-1-7394810-1-8 (Paperback)
ISBN: 978-1-7394810-2-5 (Ebook)

Cover Artwork & Design by Phoenix James.
Book Design & Formatting by Phoenix James.

Visit the author's website at www.PhoenixJamesOfficial.com or email him at phoenix@PhoenixJamesOfficial.com

DEDICATION

Forever and ever
To the freedom
And flow of thoughts
And their expression
Without limitation
Free from confinement
Judgement or restraint
Punishment and shame

To the fearlessness
Of sharing and imparting
Unpopular ideas and opinions

To the courage to stand firm
In one's own personal truth
Regardless of its darkness

To remaining your own hero
Amidst all of your pain
To speaking your soul
With zero shame

And to a young boy
With so much still to say
Still profoundly amazed
And in wonderment at it all
The floor is all yours
When I grow up, if I do
I want to be just like you.

CONTENTS

A THING FOR THE OLDER WOMAN 1
ALONE ON A DESERT ISLAND 3
BEFORE YOU EVER "GET MARRIED" 9
BLACK GIRL IN MADRID 18
CAN A PERSON BE BORN EVIL? 21
CHANGE THE WORLD 22
DATING A BISEXUAL WOMAN 24
EATING HUMAN REMAINS TO STAY ALIVE 28
HAVING A ONE NIGHT STAND 33
HOUSE OF EMOTIONS 36
HOW A POEM COMES TOGETHER 42
I TOLD HER TO SWALLOW NOT SPIT 45
IF A MAN SAYS THE SEX WAS RUBBISH 49
INFLUENCER 54
KNIFE CRIME 56
MORE OF WHAT I KNOW 60
NEVER BEEN GOOD AT QUICKIES 68
NOISY SEX AND SATISFYING HER 74
ON APPROACHING WOMEN 79
PUBLIC DISPLAYS OF AFFECTION 83
SEX BEFORE MARRIAGE PLEASE 87
THE EVOLUTION OF MAN & MICROCHIP 90
THE ONLY THING FOREVER IS CHANGE 99
THE TIME I STOOD HER UP 107
TRANSCRIBING THE FUTURE 110
TWINE 113
WHEN A WOMAN CHEATS 115
WHEN LIGHT TAKES HOLD 119
WHY 122
WHY I LOVED FRIDAYS AS A KID 124
WORSHIPPING AT THE ALTAR OF HER 127
YOKE 135
YOUR AUTHOR 136

A THING FOR THE OLDER WOMAN

The oldest woman
I have gone out with
Older than me
The gap is of eleven years
That's the biggest gap
My first girlfriend
When I was sixteen
Was twenty-seven
So that's an eleven year gap
I had another girlfriend
Who was fifty
When I would have been
In my late thirties
So that's touching on
Around the same age gap
Of eleven to twelve years roughly
Now that's for older women
Younger than me
Has been very rare
I can't think of many younger
And if so
It would have been by
Only a couple of years
Three at the most

Predominantly
From a young age
I've always been attracted
To older women
And not only
Have I been attracted to them
But it has just gone that way
Throughout my life
In terms of dating
And relationships
It has always been older women
I struggle to think
Of a time or times
Where the women were younger
I know there have been times
But again
It probably wasn't thought about
Because it was only a couple of years
Here and there
Give or take
But mostly older women
The oldest being an eleven
To twelve year gap
Seems I have a thing for the older woman
Or they just have a thing for younger guys
And it just worked out for them.

ALONE ON A DESERT ISLAND

I would have to have something
That allowed me to remain creative
For sure
Pen and paper
I like to think that would be
One of the items I'd have
I need to have
Some kind of pad and pen
Hopefully that would be one item
That's a must-have for me
I definitely want to be able
To put pen to paper
Anytime I want to
Jot down my thoughts
Make a journal of some kind
Of my day
Or just write down some information
That I want to preserve
So I'd like to have
Some pen and paper to do that
Pencil and paper, whatever
Then, some form of recording device
Either just audio
Or audio and video

Like a compact camera
Definitely preferably
A compact camera
Of some kind
Or any camera
Where I could make videos
And obviously
I could record audio
Through that anyway
So I could actually
Just have the video camera
I don't need
The audio device necessarily
So that's two things
I don't think I'd take a person
Because I don't know how long
I'm going to be there
I don't know how it's going to go
Because human beings are perishable
What if I'm with them
And then they die
I'm taking them away
From where they safely were before
That's a tough one
I don't know if I'd bring a person
I might be better off on my own

I haven't got to worry
I haven't got that responsibility
And they haven't got
That responsibility either
Like if there's no food
And I have to eat them
If there's no more food
Depending on how long
We are there for
I might get fed up
And want to get rid of them
They may just piss me off
They might not be able to hack it
To cope
In all honesty
Stranded on this desert island
Just me
And I've got enough food
I've got enough water
And I've got shelter
And I'm warm
I think under those circumstances
I would be on my own
I'd stay on my own
I wouldn't take anyone with me
I feel it would be an empowering

Spiritually uplifting
Growth experience
That would be best experienced
On my own
I think what I would become
From that experience
Whether it's six months
Or it's a year
I would treat it like a retreat
Like a personal solitary retreat
Self discovery
All of that good stuff
I think I would
Take advantage of that
That time to be alone
Man and nature
And not have
Another human around at all
Just me and the elements
And just get so in tune with myself
That I just arrive at another place
That I've never even been to
Within myself
And go on that journey
And because I wonder
If I could do it

If it's even possible
If I'd be lonely
Is the whole reason
Why I would do it
Or should do it
Because of that doubt
That I would be on my own
And could I survive
Or how would it be on my own
And all those lonely nights
And who to talk to
I think that would be
So empowering
To go through it
And experience it
Self discoveries
Solitude
Silence
That would be amazing I think
I think because you don't have
Anyone to interact with
I think you would have so much
Interaction with yourself
That it would just be another world
Some may say
That the solitude

Would maybe
Make you go crazy
But then who's there to say
That you're crazy
Who's there to diagnose you
You'd be in your bliss
I just believe
You'd arrive at such a place
That would be so beautiful
To see and experience
That I would definitely
Think strongly about going
Or being on my own
Even if I had a choice
To take a person
I would be very inspired
To go alone
One hundred percent.

BEFORE YOU EVER "GET MARRIED"

I would do away with marriage
I would do away with
The social construct
Of marriage
I would do away with it
I would do away
With putting a ring on the finger
Ceremony
Church wedding
Wedding dress
Bride
Groom
Bridesmaids
Telling grandmother to get a new hat
We're getting married
I'd do away with all of that
Wedding cake
I'd get rid of all of that
And I would replace it with
Marriage of the mind
Body
And soul
Between two individuals
And then

If that was solid and true
And real
And genuine
Marriage of the mind
Body and soul
Between those two individuals
Then I'd bring the other part back
After that first part
Has been taken care of
Then they could go
And put on a pretty dress
And say they're going to celebrate it
And have bridesmaids
And invite grandmother
With her brand new hat
And have their pretty cake
In whatever remote place
They want to do it
On a nice beach somewhere
Or wherever
All the guests wearing white
Whatever they want to do
However they want to have it done
I would grant that
But not until
The real marriage

The important marriage
Which is
The union of the individuals
Not before that
I think real marriage
Is a union of two people
Who are connected fully
Who are unified in those areas
Mentally they connect
Physically they connect
Spiritually they connect
Often marriage ends
And breaks up
And collapses
Because it's not a real marriage
It's not a real marriage
Of those individuals
It's a real marriage in the sense
That they spent a lot of money
Announced it to everyone
Stood in front of people
Said vows to each other
Bought some jewellery
Got a cake
Signed the paperwork
And did all of that stuff

But there was no real marriage
There was no real
In depth existence
Of what marriage
Is supposed to be really about
That didn't exist
So after the ceremony
After all the hoo-ha
It was on its decline
It was on its way down after that
Because that was
All they thought it was about
They didn't think about
What the marriage is really about
And the fact that it takes work
And there has to be a connection
It's all fine and well to go and do that
But how long is it going to last
Without the rest of it
There needs to be a real union
A real marriage
Of the two individuals
And marriage does not mean
A wedding day
The wedding day should be
The celebration

Of finding and discovering
That you've found yourself married
To someone
And them married to you
And this is before any ring
And all the rest of the stuff
That you do on that day
When you say I do
I don't think enough people
Think about that aspect of it
I think they think about
How nice it will be
To have a wedding day
I think they think about that
And everything that would be involved
Before it and after it
The actual day
The honeymoon
The preparation leading up to it
I don't think they think about
Everything else outside of that
Deeply
I think it's based on
How those two individuals feel
Because this is the problem
We talk about getting married

You should already be married
To the person
That you're celebrating that big day with
I see a wedding day
As a celebration of something
That should already exist
You don't get married
You should already be married
That day should be a celebration
Of what you already have
It should be someone
That you want to be with
And around
All the time
Like you've got to a point of
You feel something is missing
When you're not around them
For a specific period of time
That would be a part of
Being married to somebody
I don't mean being married
As in having a ring on your finger
I mean being married
Connected spiritually
And emotionally
And mentally

The marriage has to be in your head
It has to be in your heart
It has to be in your actions
It has to be in your soul
Everything you do
Would have to be
Considering that person
That would be a marriage
A marriage is
When a woman has a child
That's a marriage
When a family has a child
That's a marriage
Or at least it should be
A real marriage
Is something that would exist
Without getting married
A real marriage is something
That already exists
Without getting married
Without a wedding day
And would exist
Even without that wedding day
That's what a marriage is
That's what a real marriage is
It would exist

Even if that person
Didn't get down on their knee
That person didn't say yes
That person didn't place a ring
On the other one's finger
It would still be a marriage
That's what a real marriage is
All the rest of it is just airy-fairy
I could put a ring
On someone's finger
And call it a marriage
It doesn't mean it is
I could set up the wedding
And do all the stuff
Have the helicopter fly in
All fancy
And everyone's dressed in white
And on the sunny beach
I could propose to her
In some fancy way
And everyone thinks
Wow, look at that
I wish that was me
I could do all that
But none of that makes it a marriage
None of that makes it a real marriage

Not at all
What that should be
Is a celebration
Of something that already exists
A marriage that already exists
Already was
Whether it's fifty years
Whether it's five years
Or whether it's a year
It should already exist
Before we say we're getting married
If we're getting married
And we're spending all that money
We shouldn't be
We should already be married
If we're doing that
Let's get married, Let's get married
Yes, we should get married
No, you should already be married
Before you do
Whatever you're about to do
It's crazy
It's a bit crazy to me
It's just an act
It's all just an act.

BLACK GIRL IN MADRID

Why are you here
Where are you going
Don't tell me
I want to know
But I don't
I want to know you
But I won't
This will be
Our finest moment together
Forever
Meeting
But not meeting
While waiting
In transition
Never speaking
You don't need a name
Neither do I
Your face will do
Just fine
Like the rest of you
Right here
Just like this
We'll already
Have known each other

And grown each other
In love
And testimony
For a lifetime
By the time we depart
To take flight again
We'll already have
Travelled universes together
We'll already have formed
An unbreakable bond
An unshakeable sacred union
An untainted
Unattainable matrimony
As we both together
Stroll separately
Down an aisle
Respectively
Complete strangers
Yet our loving beautiful children
And their children
And their children's children
Were all birthed right here
Of this passion
In this now
This passing
Fleeing and fleeting

Transitional
Now
You'll move through time
My lover
My girlfriend
My wife
A mother
A grandmother
A goddess
As beautiful as today is
And ageless
Like cherished memories
I will too
And I love you like this
I hope we'll never meet
I hope that we'll never speak
So that we'll never have to hear
Or ever have to see
That we
Were never all
Each other hoped we would be.

CAN A PERSON BE BORN EVIL?

No, I don't think anyone is born evil at all
I think our nature is inherently good
When a baby comes into the world
I think all behaviours are learnt
I think our nature however is good
I think all behaviours after that are learnt
Based on what environment you are in
I think if you're in a good environment
It's more than likely
You're going to become good too
You're going to be a good person
I wouldn't say that they were born evil
I would say that whatever it was
In their environment
Affected them
Like growing up
Let's go back to their childhood
How they were brought up
Not even necessarily their own parents
But influences around them
And things they went through
And how did that affect them.

CHANGE THE WORLD

What would I change
Probably some of the cliche stuff
I'd definitely do it
Because it's just good to do
And it's in my heart to do it
I'd end world hunger
And poverty
And war
Those three
I end those in one go
That's poverty
Hunger
War
I would evenly distribute
The wealth of the world
So everybody had
What they needed
And more
I think there's more than enough
Wealth in the world
For everybody
For each person to have
What they need and more
So I would do that

That would mean
There would be no hunger also
And I think
That also would mean
There'd be no war
And if there was still war
And hunger
I'd end that too
But I think the first one
Would take care of the rest
I like to think so
Then again
Some people are just greedy
So yeah
I'd just end the three of those
Done
Poverty
Hunger
And war
End them
Finished
Kaput
And let everybody
Have abundance.

DATING A BISEXUAL WOMAN

I'd personally opt against
Going out with a woman
Who is into women as well as men
I think it's just too confusing
And there's just too many politics
I think there's enough politics already
When you're going out with someone
I think we all
Even those who don't admit it
Have that territorial thing
About the person
You're in a committed
Endeavour with
So if you've got other people
Who come into that space
There's a lot of animal to us
Territorial
It's there
Whether we choose to admit it or not
When another person of your sex
Comes into the space of your partner
Who could be
Of potential interest to them
Or attracting

Like how the animals work
Like that territorial thing
We very much have that
As humans too
And I think
When your partner
Is into both sexes
It then makes it double
Because it broadens
That territorial thing
Whatever that is
It makes it wider
Because you've got both
Male and female
Coming into that
So whoever they talk to
Whoever comes into that space
It won't just be females
It's also males as well
So they're coming from both sides
It's a lot
So would I go out with someone
Who is into both sexes
Who's bisexual for example
I'd probably avoid it
If I can

If I my wild hormones
Don't make me do otherwise
Or think otherwise
Where the attraction powers
Completely overtake me
And I can't control myself
Other than for that
I would definitely opt out
Of going out with someone
Who was bisexual
Because I can be jealous
I can be that person saying to myself
Who's that man talking to her
And if I've got to be like that
With women as well
Who's that woman talking to her
It's just too much
So I'd probably avoid it
I've got a little bit of that
Jealous thing going on
So I probably should avoid
Doing a double whammy on myself
With somebody who is bisexual
Who's interested in both
Men and women
That's just too much

But then
Is that me then not trusting them
Thinking that they're someone
Who's going to be seduced
By these advances
That they may receive
From either men or women
I don't know
That's all politics as well
But I definitely
Would avoid it if I can
Then that way I've just got
Less to worry about
Basically.

EATING HUMAN REMAINS TO STAY ALIVE

Okay, so
The plane I was on has crashed
There's no food where I've crashed
All that's left is human flesh
The living have passed away
Everyone's dead
No survivors but me
All that's left
Is human flesh to salvage
To cut up to cook and eat
I'm not killing anybody
They're already dead
I'd be thinking survival
And if there's nothing else
For me to eat
Those people are dead already
And it's a case of me surviving
To live life
To continue living
Would I do it
Or would I just die
I kind of feel in myself
That it would be stupid
To not have a piece of thigh

To keep me alive
To cut it up and cook it
I hope I have the option to cook it
Because raw would be a thing
That would be a stretch
I might just say
Let me just die with them
Because that might be a big stretch
To eat the flesh raw
I don't know
But if I can cook it
And it's there
I don't have to kill them
And they're not going to be
Much use to anyone anyway
I would think about having it
To prolong my life
Until I eventually get saved
Or someone comes to rescue me
From wherever I am
I wouldn't be opposed to it
If it was the last thing for me to eat
Before I died because of hunger
I think I would eat it
I think I would have a bit of thigh
A bit of forearm

Whatever meat it was
I think I would have to do it
So with the ability
Or facilities to cook it
Like say if I've got a fire
Well then that'll be me
I'll be having some booty on the fire
And that's a vegetarian saying that
Imagine this
You did that for so long
On this island
Surviving
Off of these dead bodies
I don't know
What you would do
To stop them all decaying
Because they're going to be decaying
You're going to have to probably
Eat quickly
Or just try and preserve them
In some way
I don't know how you would do that
Perhaps you could cook the meat
And preserve it that way
But just imagine
Over a period of time

You were eating these bodies
You had been eating human meat
For so long
That it was all you wanted
To eat afterwards
Even after you were rescued
You just had a taste for that
Just human flesh
Wow, can you imagine
That would be crazy
You probably would get back
Into eating normal sausages again
Bacon, beef, lamb, fish
Whatever type of meat you eat
And chicken and stuff
You probably would
As you got back into normal life
But just imagine
That's what you wanted
You just had that taste for that
That'd be wild
Apparently
There are some people
Who like the taste of human meat
And eating brains
Speaking of eating brains

I watched Hannibal
On TV the other day
Where he cuts open the guy's head
Takes the top part of his head off
Exposing his brain
All while the guy is still alive and awake
But seemingly sedate
And can't feel anything
Not really aware of what's happening
He cuts out a small portion of the brain
And the guy is still talking away
As he cooks it in a pan next to him
And then feeds it to him
Feeds him a piece of his own brain
Wow, that was crazy
Maybe I'd have some brains on the boil
Over the fire
Some cooked human brains
Enjoy that
And stay alive.

HAVING A ONE NIGHT STAND

I couldn't recall the number
Of one-night stands
I think in losing my virginity
As a young teenager
And liking sex
I definitely wasn't against
The odd one-night stand
Here and there
I definitely racked up a few
During that time
I couldn't give a number
Let's say
It was more than five for sure
Like, you know
People say
I can count them on one hand
And all that rubbish
I definitely couldn't count them
On my hands
I'd run out of fingers very quickly
I couldn't say a number
But it's definitely been a few
I don't think they're a bad thing to have
A one-night stand is a one-night stand

There's so many different nuances to that
Like, you know, what's involved
Was it consensual on both parts
That kind of thing
I think with two single people
Who are consenting adults
There's nothing wrong with that
I think if they're consenting
And honest
About what they're doing
And why they're doing it
Without taking the fun out too much
No contracts and all of that
On the first night
I think it's okay
I don't see anything wrong with it
A one-night stand is a one-night stand
As long as people are consenting
And they're honest
If they're asked a question
About what this is
And they both understand that
Then I think
There's nothing wrong with it
Have as big of a one-night stand
As you want

Between the two of you
I don't think there's anything wrong
Provided they're both single
And they're not hurting anyone else
Or if no-one else
Is likely to be hurt by it
I think it's fine
One-night stand away
If you're both
One-night stand advocates
And you're not going against
Anyone's beliefs
Between the two of you
Then it's fine.

HOUSE OF EMOTIONS

Someone asked me
Or it came up
In conversation
Years ago
And it's how I interpret
That whole thing
Why women
Get more
Emotionally involved in sex
Than men
Men can just
Come and go
Excuse the pun
And women tend to
Have this attachment
It's more of an emotional undertaking
Having sex with someone
I find that it's like this
Imagine a house
Men are the givers
And women are the receivers
So let's call the woman's body
The house
And let's call the man

The visitor
The man is coming into the house
You can go into someone's house
Spend some time
And you can leave the house
Go about your business
And not think anything of it
But when you are receiving
That person
When you are the person
In the house
You own the house
You're having a guest
It's a different dynamic
Because someone has
Come into your space
They've come and sat in your chair
They've come inside
Had a cup of tea
They've come and talked with you
Expressed certain things with you
Done certain things
To your house
While they were in there
Whatever it might be
Walked all over your floor

With their shoes maybe
Or whatever they've done
They've done all that
And they've left that energy
In that space
And gone
Now it's your house
So you still have that space
To deal with
You're still in the energy
Of that space
It's still in your house
The memories of that moment
It's still all around you
And on the four walls
Everywhere you look
The energy is still there
Of the guests that you had
So you're going to have
More of an attachment
To that moment
That took place in your house
Than the visitor
Who came and just left
It's not to say
That your guest

Won't have an attachment
But you're going to have more
Because you're the person
Who received them into your house
Into your space
Your energy
Your sphere
Whatever you want to call it
Whereas the visitor
The man
Has come and gone
Yeah, he'll think about it
He'll remember
Oh, yeah, I went to that house
And this is how I felt
And this is what happened
And that was nice
I really had a good time
But he's somewhere else now
He's gone
But as the woman
You live in that house
You live in that body
So you're in that moment
Pretty much all the time
Until you have

Another visitor maybe
That's how I discussed it
Years ago
And that's how it kind of works
In my mind
Why women have
A more emotional attachment
To sex
It goes a lot deeper than that
But that's just like
A surface level way
That I look at it
It's a receiving and giving thing
Like in and out
That's how I see it
If you look at the way
A woman's body works
And childbearing
And that whole nurturing thing
There's a lot more to be said
But on a surface level
I think I'm touching something there
I'm kind of hitting it
The giving and receiving thing
The guest and the visitor
And the welcomer being the host

The host
There's a word
I think that's quite important
The woman
Is the host in that sense
The man is entering
I think that's why
There's more
Of an emotional attachment
Because she's left with that
She can still feel
That you were in her house
More than you feel
As the man
That you were in her house
So the emotion is greater.

HOW A POEM COMES TOGETHER

I keep it pretty organic
In terms of how it comes together
How a poem comes together
How a piece comes together
I don't have a set way
In which it works
It could just be a word
That triggers a thought
And then I start writing on that
Or it could just be a line
Of something that really inspires me
That came to mind
And I'll go off of that
I'll say to myself
That's just beautiful
I want to carry on
Writing in that thought
In that theme
And see where that goes
Not have an end
Just go with it
Or it could be a title
That comes to mind
Something that sounds really good

Like a couple of words
That sound good together
And I just like that
I'll think to myself
That's got to be a title of a poem
Or a story
So then I'll start writing
I'll start thinking
About what that means
What do those two words mean
What does that phrase mean
And then I'll start playing with it
In my head
Then the whole picture
Will come together
About why that has that title
What that means
And then a story flows from there
A stream of consciousness
Flows from there
And I'll just go with it
There's no set way in which it comes
It comes in different ways
It could even be a song
I could hear a song
That inspires a thought

Maybe one line in a song
And I think
Wow that's amazing
I like that
I want to expand on that
The beauty of that moment
That came from that line in that song
All the things that it conjured up for me
That's poetry to me
I want to capture that moment
By documenting it in the poem
And expanding on it
So there's that as well
There's never any one place
That it comes from
Or that I stick to
There's no
Chicken and egg thing going on
It's all over the place
It can come from anywhere
And end anywhere
The title first
Or the poem first
And then I have to think about
What I'm going to call it
It can go either way.

I TOLD HER TO SWALLOW NOT SPIT

I will tell you
A sordid story
One time
I was with a female
And, you know
We were getting down
And she was performing fellatio on me
And she was spitting out her saliva
As she was doing it
Instead of swallowing it
And I'd never experienced that before
She wasn't swallowing
She kept on spitting out her saliva
This troubled me somewhat
And I told her
Don't do that
Swallow it
Stop spitting
I actually stopped her in her tracks
And I said
No, I'm not feeling that
Don't spit out
Swallow
Like, what's that

What's this about
I'm not feeling it
And then she carried on
And she didn't do it anymore
She stopped spitting
It was fine after that
But I guess that was her practice
You know, when you're young
We were both young
But what I learned from it is
I learned about what I like
And what I don't like
What it was about it for me
Is that I found it more
Of an intimate thing
If she swallowed
It meant more
It was more of an intimate
Loving
Special thing
Than if she was spitting out
The fact that she was spitting out
Just made me feel like
She wasn't that into it
And we weren't that close
It made it all distant

And such an intimate act
It made it feel disconnected
I understood from it
That was her way of doing things
She was used to doing it like that
I'd be interested to know
How she went forward after that
She probably carried on
How she would normally, I guess
I think we even discussed it
She wasn't used to any other way
That was her practice
To spit out
Not swallow
As she was in the act
As she was doing it
But I just wasn't feeling it
I've never had an orgasm that way
I've never come from oral sex ever
So I don't know what that's like
It's fine for me
If she doesn't want to swallow cum
And she wants to spit that out
That's fine
I don't mind that so much
I mean, it would be nicer

If she swallowed it
That would add to
What I was talking about
The whole intimate thing
To feel that she
Wants a part of me
Inside her
She wants to swallow me
That kind of thing
That's nice
I wouldn't be offended
If I came
And she spat that out
But while she's doing it
During the act
No
I want all her saliva
To stay in her mouth
That's what I like
I've come to learn.

IF A MAN SAYS THE SEX WAS RUBBISH

You have to remember
Men are different
I know that much
I don't really see men to compare
In terms of genitalia
I haven't had anything
To compare it to
But hearing from women
When they're comparing me
To other men
I know there are differences
I can tell from what they say
That tells me enough information
To let me know
That all men are not the same
And you may see
A programme on TV
And you can know from that
Or from watching porn
But not every woman is the same
In the same way
That not every man is the same
A man can sleep with one woman
Who's vagina is different

Feels different
Because it's different
It's different than another woman
It may be wider
It may be smaller
It may be bigger
It may be shorter
It may be tighter
So, it's like anything
It's like crawling into a cave
The more space you've got
The more you can move around
And the less you can feel
The walls against you
So you're going be
Able to move around
And get in more
And the more
You're going to struggle
To get in
If it's a tighter entrance
How that's going to affect you
Going in
Is going to be different
Depending on
If it's one or the other

50

A man can say
The sex was rubbish
Because he didn't get the sensation
He might have done
From another woman
Who had a tighter vagina
And therefore
Is not getting pleasure from the act
As much as he would
With another woman
There could be other reasons as well
There's not just one
That's just one aspect
For example
How big is she down there
How small is she down there
How does she feel down there
When she's shaven
Or not shaven
Or very hairy
It could be like putting his dick
Into barbed wire
If she has really coarse pubic hair
There's a million different things
That's just one other possibility
But it also may be

What she's doing with her body
Is she like a sack of potatoes
Does she not move around a lot
Does she not do anything before sex
To make him even more aroused
Which makes him come even harder
At the end of it
There's different reasons
Why he could say
That the sex was rubbish
Or why the sex was good
Maybe she was swinging
From the chandeliers
And doing splits
Things that he's never even seen
Ever in his life
Maybe she could put her legs
In positions
That he could never even dream of
Before that
So that's why
He would come and say
Wow, the sex was amazing
She did this, she did that
It was amazing
It felt so good

And then there's the opposite
Where he would say
The sex was rubbish
She just was laying like a corpse
I could definitely relate to that
Men saying the sex was rubbish
Because women are different
Just like men are different
That woman may just not have
What he needs sexually
He may need that tightness
He may that hug around his penis
When he's going in and out of her
That may be the one thing
That will make him say it's rubbish
For another guy
It might be the fact that
She didn't move around much
Or another guy could say
It's because she didn't do anal
And anal might be
His number one thing
It could be various
Different reasons
Why a guy could say
The sex is rubbish.

INFLUENCER

Yes
I would call myself an influencer
I didn't for a long time
I didn't when I first heard the word
And looked up
The definition of the word
To other people
But I came to learn that I am
And I kind of always have been
I think you are an influencer
Whenever you are doing something
That has an influence
Even if only on one person
There's so many different forms to that
In terms of online
When you talk about
An online influencer
Or someone
On the internet in that way
It tends to be about someone
Who has a big following
In whatever the thing is
That they're influencing people in
But it's so much bigger than that

It's not about
How many followers you have
And it's not only related to the internet
Someone who stands up
In front of a room of people
And has something to say
And influences their thoughts
Is an influencer
Or someone who is at home
Teaching their kids the right way
Or the wrong way
Is an influencer
An artist
Puts up a painting
In an art gallery
And people come
They stand and they look at it
And it affects the way they think
Or a piece of music
They hear somewhere
Played by somebody
Affects their mood
Or their outlook on life
That is an influencer
It's so broad
This influencer term.

KNIFE CRIME

I think
Employing all types of methods
Like all of those shock methods
Definitely is one way
One hundred percent
Going to the hospitals
And the prisons
And talking to people
Who have done that
Who were maybe reformed
Whilst in there
And willing to talk about it
And explain
What it's like to be in prison
And let them know
Because a lot of young people
Don't really know that side of it
They know about carrying a knife
Committing the act
And all of that side
But not what it is
When they end up in jail
And all the rest of it
All the rest of the politics that go on

That's one way
And the other one
Going into the hospitals
And seeing stab victims
And what being stabbed
Has taken away from them
What they've lost
Through being stabbed
And being involved
With knives in general
And also going to the cemetery
And seeing some of those people
Who are laying there
Or not seen any more
Because they're dead
And they're in the cemetery
Visiting some of those people
Who died because of stabbing
Or through knife crime
And from that perspective as well
From the grave
I think those
Will be some good methods
To definitely employ
Regarding stabbing
And carrying around knives

And violence of that nature
I'm sure unfortunately
There are a lot of young people
Walking around with knives
Who don't really know
What the actual
Real implications are
Of stabbing someone
Or being stabbed
Or everything
That can come from that
The worse being death or prison
Being affected for life
Severely disfigured
Or paralysed for life
Because of a stab wound
Or a stabbing incident
Being stabbed
All that stuff that they've not
Really taken into account
Or just haven't been exposed to
Or just haven't seen
Or just need to see
What you're really dealing with
When you're carrying a knife
With intent to cause harm

It all too often
Has gone fatally wrong
For the person
Who was actually
The one carrying the knife
I think that is very important
To highlight
And I think
Those shock methods
And even more drastic
Thoughtfully considered
Carefully orchestrated
Dramatised ones
Would definitely go a long way
Towards possibly
Helping the situation
And making people think twice
About carrying knives
And about what they're doing.

MORE OF WHAT I KNOW

If it's creative
If you ask me about creativity
I can talk about that
I can talk about creativity and art
And anything in that arena
I can talk about
I can understand it
I can talk about it
Because I live it
I've lived it
I've always lived it
And I continue to live it
And it's my makeup
It's in my DNA
I've always been creative
From young
From a baby I've been creative
So if you're talking creativity
And all of that
I can talk
That's a conversation I can have
And I can speak
And I can stand up
And let my voice be heard

Because I know
What I'm talking about
I can take a Q&A
Because I know
What I'm talking about
I've lived it
I've experienced it
I continue to live it
I'm naturally creative
And I've always been creating
For as long as I've been alive
In many different forms
For as long as I have known myself
I talk about what I know
And I like to stick to that
You won't hear me talking
A lot about religion or politics
And stuff I don't know about
I know a bit about it
I can talk a little bit
But I'm not going to have
A debate with you
Unless I know what I'm talking about
I could talk a little bit about stuff
That I know
I've travelled

I've studied
I know things
I can talk
But I'm not going to go toe-to-toe
On any subject
I don't know enough about
I'm just not going to do it
It just doesn't make sense
But people do it
And they don't know
What the hell they're talking about
I just say, sorry I don't know
I just don't know enough on the subject
To get into stuff like that
Like that whole Brexit thing
I know a bit
I see the news
I know to a degree what's happening
I know what it's all about
But I don't really know
I couldn't actually go
And give a talk on it
To people who know the subject
And about what's going on
I would stay in my lane basically
But if I had to speak about it

Be guaranteed I would learn
What I need to know
To then go and speak to people
Because I'm thorough like that
But other than that
I stay in my lane
And talk about
The things I know about
I could talk about sex
Because I know that
I've done it
I've lived it
I've had it
Since I was fifteen years old
To the present day
I could talk about relationships
Because I've been in them
I've lived them
I've been in and out of them
I can talk about relationships
I can talk about food
Because I eat every day
I live these things
I can't talk about
Things I don't know about
I will stay away from them

It makes sense
The thing about that
Is when you see someone
Talking about a subject
That they know back-to-front
Like the back of their hand
It seems like they're so knowledgeable
They have an amazing brain
They know everything
But they seem that way
Because they're talking
About things that they know
They're talking about a thing
That they know very well
And they're passionate about
And they can tell you
The back-to-front about it
Because they live and breathe it
You ask them
About a completely unrelated subject
Like fixing a car maybe
They couldn't tell you anything
Because they know nothing of fixing cars
But the guy who does know
About fixing cars
Could talk about fixing cars

All day long
Because that's what he does
He knows that stuff
You ask him about public speaking
He wouldn't know where to start
You ask him about preparing
And baking a cake
He'd be stuck
Ask him how to change a car tyre
He could go on for hours
People who know their thing
And who can talk about their thing
Passionately
They are the best at that
You could maybe talk to someone
About changing tyres
Because you've done it
You've lived it
You've experienced it
You know what it's like
But me for example
If you spoke to me
About changing a car tyre
I wouldn't know where to start
I've seen it done
Because my mum has done it

I've seen her do it
But I couldn't tell you how
I wasn't at the time
Paying enough attention
To tell you now what to do
And run you through it
And the whole process
She could
And that's what's important
When people talk about
Staying in your lane
That's where you shine most
You shine by staying in your lane
Let me focus on
And talk about
What I know
There's nothing I talk about
Where I don't know
What I'm talking about
And if I do come to something
That I don't know what I'm talking about
That I have to talk about
I'll say I don't know a lot about it
But this is what I do know
Or at least this is what I've heard
I have no problem

With saying I don't know
Because I really
Don't know everything
I'll be the first to put my hands up
And say I don't know
I really don't know
I don't know enough
About that subject
This is the little bit I know
Or this is the bit I've heard
Or this is what my friend says
Who is an expert in the field
I'm not going to be up there
Saying I know it
When I don't know it
For example
A random thing
Climate change
I know what it is
But I couldn't educate you on it
I don't know enough
The ins and outs of it
When I say the ins and outs
I mean the intricate parts of a thing
I know what it is
But I couldn't sit down and school you on it.

NEVER BEEN GOOD AT QUICKIES

I like to take my time
In my ideal environment
Ideal circumstance
Ideal situation
I like to take my time
I like lovemaking
I like making love
Love creating
I like to take time
And create that stuff
I love foreplay
I like it to last
It's an event for me
I like it
I like to take my time
I like to be relaxed
In a relaxed environment
I like everything
To be as right as possible
I like it to be cosy and stuff
I mean, if it can be
That's my ideal situation
I want to be in
Which is not always ideal

That's my go-to
If I could, you know
Plan it out
And say
We're going to be doing our thing
And we'll have our little cosy set up
And the phone is going to be off
No one's going to bother us
We'll put our sexy music on
And just relax
And get into it
She's not going to be disturbed
I'm not going to be disturbed
Prepare, you know
But that's not always possible
The way the world is
And busy lifestyles
And schedules
And deadlines
And appointments
So if that's not possible
And I'm super horny
And I can't have that
I'm not going to not have it
I'm gonna take a quickie
But the problem is

I'm not good at quickies
Because my quickies are not quickies
In what I know quickies to be
It's not a thing I'm good at
A quickie is supposed to be quick
That's the idea of a quickie
I've never been good at those
If that's all that's going
I'll try my best
I may still make you late
But I'll give it a go
But if I can avoid a quickie
And I can enjoy myself
And make love
And foreplay
And all that stuff
I prefer that
That's great
But if I have to have it quick
And we haven't got a choice
And we were in a hurry
And we're not going to get it otherwise
And I don't think I want to wait
Then I'm going to take the quickie
And then you just have to hope
That I'll be quick

Forty-five minute quickies
Because I'm so used to taking my time
I just like to be relaxed
I like to enjoy it
What am I rushing for
It's not a thing that should be rushed
Why would you be rushing
Sex is enjoyable
Sex is fun
Sex is erotic
It's sensual
It's supposed to take time
It's supposed to be special
You put out stuff
Whatever things add to it
Your candles
Whatever aroma you're going to have
Whatever music you're going to have
Whatever you're going to wear
However you're going to present yourself
You spend time preparing
Imagine a woman now
She goes and gets her hair done
She's got a date
She's meeting this guy
She knows very well

Things are going to go down
Hair done
Face done
Nails done
Legs done
Feet done
Toes done
All that
Gets a wax
Waxes all her bits
Gets all smooth for the man
And makes him a nice meal
Or goes out shopping
Goes and gets the outfit
She wants to wear
Lingerie
She does all of that preparation
And then
When they get down to it
It's just a rush-rush thing
And it's like over in five minutes
She's not going to be happy
I mean, he might be fine
But not her
It's supposed to be a thing
Where you take time

It's supposed to be sensual
And slow
But in saying that though
Some women I've spoken to
They want it rough and ready
But even then
They still want it to last a while
Some do like it rough
But even those women
Don't want it over too quickly
To be over in two seconds
So even then
They still want it
To take some time
They still want to get
Some pleasure out of it
Prolonged pleasure
Not like two-second pleasure
So even those women
Want it to take time
And I'm of that nature as well
I like to take my time
I enjoy foreplay a lot
I enjoy taking my time
If it's nice
You just want it to last.

NOISY SEX AND SATISFYING HER

It's dependent on the environment
But for the most part
I like when a woman is making noise
Making some kind of verbal sound
I've had women just laying
Like a sack of potatoes
I can definitely compare it
To when a woman
Is actually physically
And verbally
Showing her enjoyment
That's great
I prefer that
I like when a woman is noisy
Obviously, that's if I'm the one
Who is actually making her noisy
And she's not putting it on
If I'm making her respond that way
That's a big turn on
I prefer that
Than the sack of potatoes
One hundred percent
I mean, who wouldn't
That's going to turn the person on

To know that they are
Giving someone else pleasure
And they're expressing it verbally
I'm all for the screaming
And the 'You're killing me'
In a good way
And depending
On the environment
It's fine
I mean, if you've got a relative
In the next room
An older relative
It then might not be so good
To be screaming down the place
Especially if it's perhaps
Some Christian churchgoer
Maybe your aunt
Or your mum
It's probably not going to be good
That he or she can hear
Screams of sexual pleasure
Coming from the next room
So it's all based on environment
If it's a hotel room
Then yes, go for it
Scream the whole building down

Let every room in that hotel
Hear you
I'm fine with that
But maybe not in your aunt's house
I'm relatively quiet myself
In contrast
Yeah, I'm quite quiet
Depending on the moment
I've never screamed out
I've been verbal
But the majority of the time
I'm relatively quiet in comparison
To the woman
Who is screaming down the room
I guess I'm concentrating
I'm concentrating on what I'm doing
And enjoying it at the same time
Which sometimes
Could make the other person
Unsure whether I'm enjoying it
I've had that in the past
And it kind of made me aware
Of the necessity
To express that I'm enjoying it
At the same time
So that they're aware

That I'm enjoying it
As much as they are
Because obviously
I'm less noisy
Or less verbal
But I think
I'm generally quiet anyway
And also I'm concentrating
On what I'm doing
I want to hit all the marks
So we both get to
Where we need to go
There's times I've realised
I'm might come
Quicker than I want to
And I've focused my mind
On something else
And it slows me down
Or I'll stop for a while
I'll stop for a moment
And I'll do something else
I'll keep her entertained
In another way
And then I'll go back to it
And everybody's happy
Or what I've done is

I've just come
And then entertained her further
Because I'm just too proud
My ego wouldn't allow me
To have her saying
That she wasn't pleasured
That she wasn't entertained
Not to say
That she's going go tell people
But I mean, in my mind
And in her mind
It wouldn't sit well with me
Knowing that she's thinking
She didn't enjoy herself
Or she didn't climax
She wanted to
But she didn't
She's not satisfied
That wouldn't satisfy me
Knowing that I didn't satisfy her
So I would actually
Work above and beyond
To make sure
That she came harder than I did
That would feed my ego
Very well.

ON APPROACHING WOMEN

I've had rejection
I've had times where
I've approached girls
Or approached women
And they're not open
To my advances
I think
Every guy pretty much has
Who has gone out
And put himself out there
To approach a female
Or male
If that's his persuasion
It's putting yourself out there
And then getting knocked down
It's never going to be a great feeling
It's all about your ability
To take it on the chin
And move on to the next one
Without thinking
It's the end of the world
I'm probably one of the guys
That would be affected by it more
Because I'm quite a shy person

Whereas you've got guys
Who would just go out
And could get twenty No's
And they're still going
They're not even fazed
The girl could ridicule them
In the most terrible way
Like, who do you think
You're talking to
You're beneath me
Get away from me
All that kind of stuff
And the guy just moves on
As if it didn't happen
Onto the next one
Like they could take
A thousand rejections
And not be fazed by it
I'm not so much like that
I wish I was
I'd probably do more
Of the approaching
If I was more like that
But I'm just not that way
I'm just not wired that way
I'm confident

In something I'm familiar with
That I'm in control of
Something I know
It's an arena that I'm familiar with
And I know what I'm doing
And I'm comfortable in it
When you're approaching a stranger
It's a whole different thing
You don't know
What you're getting yourself into
It's not like when I go on stage
And I know what I'm getting into
So I can't really compare
Performing on stage
To approaching a woman
I don't know
If it's the type of person you are
Or if it's the amount
Of practice you've had
If you've done it
A thousand times
Then it's going to be like nothing
Which I guess
Is like the performing for me
I know it
And I know

That I'm comfortable with it
Maybe I haven't done it enough
Maybe I haven't put myself out there
To approach women enough
I don't know if shy is the right word
But it would take more for me
To do that
Than it would for me to go on stage
In front of hundreds
Or thousands of people
Because I've done that
Hundreds of times
It will take more for me to approach
A singular woman
Or a small group of women
It would require more of me to do that
I'd have to psych myself up more
More than I would
To go on stage and present myself
In front of a mass of people
True story
But in actuality now
Having thought about it more
I know exactly why that is
Why I've found approaching harder
I just simply haven't done it enough.

PUBLIC DISPLAYS OF AFFECTION

Okay.. PDA
Public Display of Affection
I'll tell you what
I like PDA
I like public displays of affection
But I am also
Quite a private person
Contrary to popular belief
But I like them
And I don't like them
So I would choose my moment
To have a public display
Of affection
It's when I feel comfortable
Or just when the energy takes me
It just has to be right for me
To kind of be in that moment
And there's other times
Where I'll say
I don't want to do that
Maybe if it's a big crowd
Or something
And there's a hundred people
Around me

Maybe then
I probably wouldn't be that way
But I may be when
It's somewhere more quiet
Or even down a side street
Or on our way somewhere
And it's on the move
It depends
I haven't really analysed
Too deeply
What that's about
But I think I have my moments
When I feel cool about it
And when I don't
I genuinely do like
Doing that kind of thing
Outdoors
Which sounds crazy
But yeah
You know what I mean
I do like public displays of affection
But maybe not too public I guess
Or maybe it can be
Because the public is people
If it's a massive amount of people
It doesn't matter

Depending on my mood
But my mood may go either way
Let's say a big crowd of people
Which is the public
It could be that day
That I feel cool about it
I don't care who's around
It doesn't really matter
And it could be another day
Where I'm more conscious of it
And I'm more worried about
Who's around
And I want to be more low key
So I may wait
Until there's
Not many people around
It all depends on me
Because there's times
Where I'm cool like that
I don't care who's around
Who's seeing me
What public is there
And there are times
Where I just
Try to avoid that at all costs
And I'm not feeling

Being public
With my displays of affection
At all
So that's me on that
I think
I'm quite contradictory with it
Definitely I am
I'm a hypocrite with it
I like it when I like it
I like to think I'm not alone
I'm not strange in any way
I think everyone's the same
They have moments
They're cool to be public
And moments they're not.

SEX BEFORE MARRIAGE PLEASE

I definitely want to
Squeeze the fruit
Before I buy
One hundred percent
We're talking about
Getting married here
Talking about spending
The rest of your life
With someone
Which is what marriage
Is supposed to be about
So yeah
I want to squeeze the fruit
I want to see what I'm getting
I want to taste it
I want to strip the skin off
And get it right inside
To the root of it
To the seed
I want to experience
Every aspect of that fruit
In that department
Before I buy
Definitely

I don't see
Anything wrong with that
I think that makes sense
To me
I get it
People arrange marriage
And have all these beliefs
About not experiencing
That part of the person
Before you get married
But me personally
If I'm speaking for myself
I definitely want to know
What I'm getting
Before I actually get it
I definitely want to see
What's going down
In that department
Excuse the pun
I definitely want to get down
And see what's what
What's happening
And what needs to be worked on
And see if it can be worked on
And work on it
Long before

We purchase the tree
Because if you've purchased the tree
And nothing is growing on it
Then you've just got a tree
That's just a tree
That is just nice to look at
A tree that is lovely to look at
But it's not going to
Bear you any fruit
That you're going to enjoy
The sweetness of
I want to enjoy the sweetness
Of that tree by tasting its fruit
Before I commit myself
To owning it
Yes indeed
I want to sample it first.

THE EVOLUTION OF MAN & MICROCHIP

I'm coming from
A certain generation
My parents are coming
From another generation
And my grandparents
Came from another generation
In terms of microchipping
It's like we already have the chip
We already have it
We have a version of it already
And we always have
It's just been an evolution of us
And an evolution
Of what that chip is
I feel like credit cards
Were a form of chip
I feel like cash
Was a form of chip
Evolution
From cash to credit cards
To then Contactless
Is a form of chip
I feel it's all a process of preparation
We were talking

About the London buses
And it not being possible
To board one with cash anymore
You have to have an Oyster card
Call that card a chip
Every card has a chip
I feel that's a stage in the evolution
And preparation for what's to come
This whole cashless society
That we hear about so often
I feel the chip is already here
It's all just preparing us for
Not having to have a physical thing
That you're carrying around
I believe in a time
Where you won't even actually
Have to carry around a credit card
And you won't have to have
A contactless card
For transactions anymore
Not very long ago
You always used to have to
Put your card into a machine
And type in some digits
And now you can actually just tap
Or hover the card over a point

And all the information is there
And you make your transaction
I feel there will come a time
Where you won't even have to do that
With any physical thing
Apart from your own hand
Or your eye
Or your finger tip
I feel it will just be a part of your body
That will be the next stage in the evolution
It will be something that's implanted in you
Where you don't have to carry a phone
You don't have to carry a credit card
Where you don't have to carry anything
That has the credit on it
Or has the ability on it to do what you need
You will be able to do it with your own body
Because you will have that thing
That technology
Or that intelligence
Inside of your body
I do believe a time like that will come
We've seen it with animals being chipped
They're talking about in certain countries
How people are being chipped already
It's not like a thing that's to come

There are people living and existing
With chips inside of them already
Working in this way
I'd say it's only something to come
In terms of a wider usage of it
A much bigger population
Living this way
With microchips implanted
As a normal way of life
I think there will come that time
People now don't want to carry stuff
No-one wants to have to wait on things
They want things now
It's not going to be long before
Carrying a phone will seem antiquated
Out-dated and unnecessary
They'll say
What are you carrying that for
Why are you carrying a cellphone
Why would you want to carry that
When you could be like us
You've got to charge that up
You've got to type in the numbers
That's long, man
When are you going to get your chip
Get your chip

You don't have to do any of that
That's just a waste of time, man
Why have you got a cellphone
Who carries a smartphone nowadays
That's what it's going to be like
That will be the conversation
Why have you got that credit card, man
What are you doing
Walking around with credit cards
Who does that anymore
Wow, get your chip, man
Why are you taking so long
To get your chip
That's what the conversation
Is going to be in the future
I feel it's all already in process
So when I talk about the microchip
Already being here from ages ago
Long before the conversations
Even became popular
It's just an evolution
It's preparation
Because I don't think
Anyone is willingly
Going to have a chip
Put into their hand

So there has to be a preparation
It's all gearing towards an acceptance
So whereas
I spoke about the gran
And the mum
And then the child
Who have grown up without it
You will have the generations
In the future
Their children
The children of the children
Or the grandchildren of the children
Who will be more open to it
Because they've grown up
In a world
Where they don't
Have to have a credit card
Or they don't have to type in a pin
They can tap everything
They can tap it, they can swipe it
They can voice activate it
They're being born into that world
So it's more acceptable to them
They're born into a world where
They can have a contraceptive implant
Implanted into their bodies

And that does everything fine
They don't have to swallow a pill
And there's always going to be issues
Because it's not really normal
It's not really human-like
To have something
Inserted into your body
That's artificial
That's not supposed to be there
You weren't born with it
There's problems with everything
That you implant into your body
There's always going to be issues
Of some kind
Until it works properly
There's always going to be
Teething issues
Side effects with things
That are not supposed to be inside us
The contraceptive implant
For example
A lot of people
Are already walking around with it
But think about it
It's an implant
It's amazing to think about

People are already accepting
Micro implants
So it's not that far-fetched
It may be far-fetched for us
Who are of an older generation
Who grew up seeing the change
But people that are being born into it
It's like nothing
It's all a normal thing
You can get breast implants
You can get your lips done
You can get your bum done
These are all relatively new things
If you look at history
So by the time
Those future generations get here
It'll be normal for them to have a chip
They'll say, *Where's your chip*
Why haven't you got a chip
The people who
Don't have the chip
Will be the ones
Who are looked upon
Like you're some alien
Being told to
Get with the times, man

Why haven you got a chip
They'll be saying
Who doesn't have a chip these days
You're in the stone ages
That's how they'll be talking about you
They'll be talking about you
Like you're in the stone ages
Because you've got an iPhone
That's how the future is going to be
People are going to take a look at you
With your Contactless card or device
As if you're some old person
Like you're stuck in the past
Because you're tapping your card
To pay for your items
Or to make the purchase
They'll say
Who does that anymore
I seriously think
We're going to be
Downloading everything
Into our bodies
As opposed to onto a device
I really do believe
That in the future
Such things will be just normal.

THE ONLY THING FOREVER IS CHANGE

I'm trying to think of a time
I've gone back
To a previous relationship
Like, got back with someone
That I've been with before
I'm trying to think of a time
I'm sure there is a time
There's definitely times
They were good ideas
For a time
To go back
And then a time came
Where it wasn't a good idea
To go back
It was a good idea at the time
But then it worked out that
It wasn't a good idea
Although
I can't take away from the fact
That at that time
The getting back was good
I can't take away from that
But then obviously
You're reminded

Why it didn't work in the first place
But then you kind of move on
There's been times
I've gone back
To previous mistakes
Previous relationships
That didn't work out
The second time around either
It's just the nature of it
I guess they kind of
Serve as reminders
Why it didn't work
The first time around
But I think it can't take away
From the fact
That when you did get back
At that moment
Or in that timeframe
It was good
Which is why you got back
But you're quickly reminded
That it was a bad idea
I wouldn't say
It's not a good idea to go back
Because people go back
And it's like

Happily ever after
And they kind of work out
What didn't go right the first time
Maybe that's the case
With the people
Who go back two or three times
And it doesn't work out
Even the fourth time
It doesn't work out
Maybe they just
Haven't worked out
Past that point where they fail
Or where it goes wrong
Maybe if they did
It would be okay
Or maybe they're just
Not meant to be together
You just don't know
It can go either way
I don't think it means
That you're not meant
To be together
I just think
It's dependent on
Different factors
It can work, or it can't work

You just find out
That you are not
Meant to be together
Or you work out what was wrong
The second time around
And you get it right
That second time around
Or later on
After being away
From the relationship
And realising
Where you both went wrong
You come back
And you come to that stage again
And you kind of know
What went wrong
And you don't go that way again
You both manage to get past it
And it's all happily ever after
Roses
Everybody happy
Or you're just not compatible
You just get to that same place
And you've done all the working out
And you've worked out
Where you went wrong

You tried to do it again
And it still doesn't work
And you think to yourself
You know what, nah
You're expecting things
To be a certain way
You think
That you know them so well
Or you think
You know them so well
That you think you know
What they're going to do
And you start assuming things
Before they even happen
And make up things in your mind
About what took place
In the way it did
And what this person is thinking
And make your own story up
In your head
About what you think they're about
And you may have it completely wrong
Which then causes friction
Which then causes ultimately
You not wanting
To be with each other

I think you're learning
About people
All the time
I think we're constantly learning
I don't think we ever
Really completely know a person
I think we're always
Going to be learning
New things about our partners
Going along
You're always going to be
Learning something new
I don't think you ever get to a point
Where you just know this person
Inside out, you know
To a degree
But I think you're always learning
Because we're always learning
About ourselves
We're always evolving ourselves
Always learning about ourselves
Our selves are always new to ourselves
All the time
So it makes sense
That we're going to be new
To someone else

All the time
And we should be
We should be evolving
We shouldn't be the same
To say that you know a person
That you can swear on your life
What they're going to do
In a certain situation
I don't think it's always the case
I don't think it's always
The right way of thinking
That you can kind of assume
Where this person is at
What they would do
When and where
And how
And then a lot of times
We end up getting it wrong
And ultimately
The relationship falls down
Or we decide
That's not the person
We thought it was
It's not going
How we thought it would go
And we don't want to be

A part of it anymore
We're always evolving
All the time
And that's why people grow
In and out of love
They either grow in
Or they grow out
Because we're always evolving
Sometimes it meets
Sometimes it doesn't
Sometimes the stars align
And sometimes they don't
But it's always moving
Change is the only thing
We can definitely guarantee
Stays the same
And will never change
The fact that change is happening
All the time
That's the one permanent thing
Change we can guarantee
Even for the human beings
That we would swear
We know them inside out
We're all evolving
As the world is.

THE TIME I STOOD HER UP

It's never been
One or the other
It's been either
I have or they have
Left the relationship
I can think of times
Where I left
And I can think of times
Where I was left
But I think
The majority fell on my side
In terms of the leaving
I remember one situation
Where I was young
A teenager
Secondary school
I was seeing a girl at the time
I was supposed to meet her
Before school
She would be at the bus stop
I would get off the bus
And meet her
I was just about to get off the bus
I was excited

Looking forward to meeting her
Over the whole weekend
The bus was driving up
To the bus stop
I'm looking out of the window
I see her
She's changed her hairstyle
I'm not feeling it
I don't like it at all
I stay on the bus
And leave her there
I don't think that was the end
Of the relationship
But it was definitely
The end of that day for us
I don't recall
If I even mentioned it
I don't know what happened after that
I clearly remember that day though
That was one situation
In that regard
But I don't think that was the end
Of the relationship
Actually, it might have been
But I don't think it was
I think I got over the hairstyle

After a while
I did not want to be seen with her
Looking like that
You know
When you're just young
And have crazy ideas
I just didn't get off the bus
I just stayed on the bus
And carried on going
I just hid myself
As the bus went by her
If I ever see her again
I'll tell her about it
But then again
I might not
Because I can't remember
If that was the last time
I saw her or not
She'd probably laugh about it now.

TRANSCRIBING THE FUTURE

I think about
In the future
I love the idea
Of all of the stuff
That I am recording now
In video form
Being transcribed
Into written form
Into writing
I like the idea of not knowing
What the future holds
It may be important enough
To somebody somewhere
In the future
That they actually want
To transcribe
Something I've said
And use it as a reference
I'm just in love with the idea of that
The fact that it will be there
If somebody
Should feel the need or desire
Or want to refer to it
And transcribe what's there

It's a nice thought
That it's possible
It's possible because
I've made the effort
To record it in the first place
For that to happen
That it means that much
That somebody
Would come back to it
Down the line
The things we set in motion now
Are going to have an effect
On the future
You turn left down one road
As opposed to turning right
That sets in motion
The future for everybody
Or at least
For those connected to you
Or that you come into contact with
That's amazing
Because in that sense
You are important
We have an effect on the world
Whether we like it or not
You go into a shop, for example

Your local convenience store
The shopkeeper
Behind the counter
You smile at him
Or you frown at him
It's going to have an effect
On both of you
Like how ripples work
Like energy
You can go in there and smile
And say how is your day
How are you doing
Good to see you
How's your son
Or you can go in there
And have an argument with him
It's all affective
We're affecting the world
All the time
As insignificant
As some of us think we may be
We have power
We have an effect on the world.

TWINE

Why is it seemingly
Always the married wives
Who always seem fully ready
To be the most committed
To the random single guys
They meet on these dating sites

New appealing dudes who
By now have probably seen
More nudes
And naked pictures
Of these wives
Than their husbands at home do

She claims they permanently sleep
In separate rooms
Insisting there's no attraction and no sex
Just living a lonely loveless existence
But who indeed would really know
Says she'll stay that way
Until the children grow

Perhaps it's the sad truth
Or maybe that's just the story

She has playing on repeat
To every new unsuspecting guy she meets
So that he'll be completely comfortable
When lying with her between the sheets

She'll again tell hubby this weekend
That she's going to stay with a girlfriend
When in actual fact it's far from that
She'll instead be meeting
With her new match
That she's been exchanging messages with
On the dating app.

WHEN A WOMAN CHEATS

I don't think
Any man in existence
Could ever cheat
Like a woman
Any man gone
Yet to come
Or present today
That could ever cheat
As well as a woman can
I think there's no competition
I think when a woman
Is ready to cheat
And do everything
That's required to cheat
To keep it under wraps
To conceal it
To connive
To deceive
To lie
To pull the wool over eyes
I don't think a man
Could possibly even come close
With the amount of planning
And cleverness

And genius
To pulling cheating off
I don't think a man
Has a chance in hell
Or a hope in hell
Or a hope in heaven even
Of being that good
When women wants to cheat
And they don't want
You to find out
You just can't match that
As a man
It's just not possible
It's a losing battle
You will never compete
With a woman
When she's ready to cheat
You will never pull off her tactics
As well as she can
It's just how it is
Women can cheat better
Than any species alive
Absolutely
I know from personal experience
And from the experiences of others
I know it beyond knowing it

The reasons could be numerous
Same for a man
What reason a man cheats
Is not always one reason
That could be numerous
Same for a woman
There'll be numerous
Reasons for why
I'm just saying
That when a man
Is ready to cheat
He cannot compare
To when a woman
Is ready to cheat
She will show him
How cheating is done
And you won't even know
That it's happening
That's the funny thing about it
That's how good
Women are at cheating
She will cheat
Show you how it's done
And you won't even realise
That she's doing it
In your face

And men can't pull that off
I haven't seen them do it yet
They might think they're doing it
But women do it so well
That she knows you're cheating
She's cheating too
But she's cheating
Ten times better than you
So the fact that you're cheating
Doesn't even really matter
And she's just cool as a cucumber
That much I've learned
In my humble forty plus years.

WHEN LIGHT TAKES HOLD

I don't know what happened
But I haven't been the same
Since the day I saw you again
You've been on my mind since then
Like the last time we laid eyes
How indeed time flies
Like speeding light
Is fleeting like life
But in this brief moment
It's like slow motion
Ultra bright
And much clearer to see
That you're the type of woman
That others desire to be
Not only because of beauty
But just to experience
Being the type of woman
That grown men are inspired
To write poems of
Your hold is like home
Inviting me inside
Lingering and familiar
Like a love poem
I capture your eyes

Remembering me
Like someone you've known
Wrapped up in your energy
Mood and tone
Your frequency
Speaks to me
Pleasingly
And I'm pleased to see
That all is as it seemed to be
Back then
Is still now
Moving in time
Never stayed
But stays
Even now
I feel it as we embrace
The poetry of this moment says
You've been holding me for decades
In a place
Valued and safe
Where things don't decay
As time slowly fades away
Like a precious memory
I've held you too
In this same way
So many things I could say

Words I could write
About the beauty of your smile alone
They would fill an entire page
Woman of warmth and intelligence
Sophistication and elegance
The storm behind the scenes
Pulling all the strings
From way back when
And your smooth chocolate skin
Is as beautiful now
As it was then
Without words
You prove that she wasn't wrong
And was right to be mad
She saw clearly
Better than I did
The chemistry we had
Those early days
Before we all parted ways
We through destiny
Meet again
What's meant to be
Is meant to be
It's still crazy to believe
I haven't seen your face
In a quarter of a century.

WHY

I think it's more
Than one thing
I think the family unit has changed
Whereas it was more common
For family to raise a child
As opposed to a single parent
And that whole thing
It's not a new thing
Raising a child as a single parent
But I do believe
There was more of a unit before
That dynamic has changed
I think a lot of things
Have caused that change
I think the world has sped up
In terms of
People wanting things now
And they have access
To things right now
The internet
Being exposed
To vast amounts
Of imagery
And information

All at one time
And all that comes with it
I think it has changed
The way the world works
People are growing faster
They're have more exposure
To other things now
They're being raised
By a computer screen
As opposed to
By their parents
And doing
The old-fashioned things
That parents would do
With their children
And the rest of the family
Getting involved
When there was an issue
With a child
And that kind of thing
I think there's
So many dynamics
As to why
Our young people
Are the way they are today.

WHY I LOVED FRIDAYS AS A KID

I'll tell you
How much I love trainers
When I was in Barbados
And I used to go to school
On Fridays
You were allowed
To wear trainers
Only on Fridays
So I always looked forward
To Fridays
To put my trainers on my feet
So when you say
You don't see me in trainers
Or you're not used to me in trainers
I wear trainers when I can
When I don't have to
Wear smart shoes
I'm in trainers
It depends on the mood I'm in
But I love trainers
Because trainers are good
Friday was the day in school
I was allowed to wear trainers
The whole school could wear trainers

On Fridays
And that was a big thing
I used to have these trainers
I used to wear
A fusion of red
Black
Yellow
And white trainers
Multicoloured type trainers
I just used to look forward
To Fridays
Because I could wear my trainers
I used to love that
That was a big thing as a kid
I think I still have that now
That excitement with them
But then there's times
That I don't like trainers
There's a time
I want to be smart purposely
I want to not wear trainers
I want to wear my shoes
I love tanned shoes
I especially love tanned shoes
Or tanned boots
That's my thing

But other times
I want to wear trainers
It all depends on my mood
What I'm feeling like
On the day
I just remember Fridays
That was trainers day in school
That was the best.

WORSHIPPING AT THE ALTAR OF HER

I genuinely think
You're missing out
On a little piece of heaven
And I hope that
You get to sample that
At some stage in your life
Very soon
No way am I laughing at you at all
I'm laughing because of what I said
I said, sometime in your life
And then I said, very soon
Because, really
I think sometime in your life
Could be ten years from now
I feel the need
For you to experience
That piece of heaven much sooner
Why should you have to wait
Until you're in a nursing home
To taste some pum-pum
I just find it interesting
That you've been in five
Long term relationships
A minimum of six years each

You've been with all of those women
That you've been with
And each of those women
Have gone down on you
But you've never gone down on them
And you've never experienced
Going down on a woman at all
Ever in your life
When I look at myself
I just find that really amazing
That just blows my mind
Looking at myself and comparing it
It's like, Wow
Never tasted the fruit of life
Wow, man
It is what it is
I mean, not every man
Has gone down on a woman
I guess that's the way it is
It's just a different world
For me, it's a part of lovemaking
It's a part of foreplay
It's a natural thing
I've always been that way
When I lost my virginity
With the person I was with

That was the regular thing
Going down on a woman
Is like an experience
That is life changing
Because you get to experience
Another side of what it's like
To give a woman pleasure
To be at the seat of that pleasure
And it's a pleasure given in a way
That she cannot give to herself
And it's a beautiful thing
To be in a moment
Where you're the one
Providing that pleasure
It's a different experience
I highly recommend it
Worshipping
At the altar of the woman
That's what it's like
It's like kneeling before God
It's very empowering
Very enriching
A very spiritual experience
Along with, obviously
Physical pleasure
There's a lot going on

When you lay
Between a woman's thighs
And bow to her in that way
It's one experience
That every person should have
At least once in their lifetime
I recommend a lot more
Than just once
But at least once
It's important
I mean, don't just
Go out and do it
Just for the sake of doing it
But hopefully
You're intimate
In that way with someone
Where that can transpire
During the time that you
Both are intimate together
I'm not saying to go out
And pull someone off the street
Declaring
I have to do this
Before I die
I mean, of course
One could do that

I'm sure somebody
Would take you up on it too
Or it could go the other way
You could get a slap
You could get arrested
A lot of things could develop
So be careful
But I'm sure that at the same time
You'd have a few volunteers
Running up to you
Saying
Me, me, I will
But I definitely recommend
Experiencing it
Stop being selfish
Stop thinking about
Just your needs
You'll be a changed man
After you've prayed
To the altar of her
Get down on your knees
And worship
At the altar of her
I've also heard
I don't want to admit
That I know it's true

So I'll say I've heard
That everything
Tastes sweeter after that
After that experience
Your food tastes sweeter
Your lovemaking is sweeter
The kisses are sweeter
Your bath is sweeter
Everything is sweeter
The conversations are sweeter
Just imagine
How much sweeter everything will be
It'll be nice to experience
Not having to
Run your own bathwater for once
Home cooked food is much sweeter
Than microwaved food, my friend
That's always been my thing
I get more out of giving pleasure
Than receiving pleasure
Obviously I get a lot out of receiving
Let's be real
But I also get an extreme amount
From giving pleasure as well
Which is why I enjoy
Providing oral sex

Giving to a female
It's selfish in a lot of ways
It's a bit of a selfish act
Because I'm doing it to receive also
I mean, if I didn't enjoy giving it
As much as I do
I don't know if I would even do it
But I happen to love it
So I'll never know
What it's like not to
Generally, it's the precursor
To getting down
It lets the floodgates open
It makes all the blood flow
Much more smoothly
Around the body
Everything seems to
Work easier after that
It's like oiling something
That was creaking
And then it all suddenly
Just works so smoothly
Like it's brand new
It's a bit like that
It's oiling the cogs
It's to get things running

It's been a while now
So I've learned a few bits
I had a lot of practice
I can definitely say
I'm not rusty
It's interesting
It's one department
I could give my ten pence on
Having some experience
I definitely call myself
A seasoned expert in the field
Practice makes perfect, my friend
Practice makes perfect
I'm proud to worship
At the altar of her
I miss it at the moment
Because I'm a single man
Not experiencing that right now
That pleasure
At this present time
But I am faithful
That I will get to worship
Once again
At the altar of her
Her being
The female species.

YOKE

Sometimes
You're just
Not interested
To spend the energy
Or waste the time
Mentally
Psychologically
Reliving the trauma
Of passed moments
You've long survived
By recalling
The events
Of that time
Inside of a story
For an ear and mind
Not fully equipped
Or openly prepared
To receive
Or understand
The truths
They'll never face
Or comprehend.

ABOUT THE AUTHOR

Phoenix James is an award winning Writer, Poet, Author and Spoken Word Recording Artist. He began performing his poetic words live on stages across the UK in 1998. His debut spoken word poetry album, *The A.R.T.I.S.T,* was released in 2000. His first limited edition printed collection of poetry, *To Whom It May Concern,* was published in 2003. He has toured and performed his poetry internationally since 2004. He has appeared in films, on television and radio shows, and collaborated with other artists, singer-songwriters, actors, musicians, filmmakers and producers. In 2013, he wrote, directed and produced the feature length mock documentary film, *Love Freely but Pay for Sex.* Phoenix James is the author of several poetry collections and has recorded and released several spoken word poetry albums including *Phenzwaan Now & Forever, A Patchwork Remedy for A Broken Melody, FREE, Haven for the Tormented, With All That Said, Light Beams from the Void,* and over sixty spoken word poetry singles. All are available online now and streaming everywhere worldwide.

If you enjoyed reading this book, please leave a review or comment online. The author reads every review and they help new readers discover his work.

136

PHOENIX JAMES

Photo by Phoenix James

Phoenix James lives in London, England.

Connect with Phoenix James on his online social media platforms via www.linktr.ee/ Phoenix_James and say you've read this book. To contact or learn more about Phoenix James and his creative journey or to receive updates via his Newsletter Mailing List, visit his official website at www.PhoenixJamesOfficial.com

Phoenix James Official

www.ingramcontent.com/pod-product-compliance
Lightning Source LLC
Chambersburg PA
CBHW021235090426
42740CB00006B/551